Are You Nobody?

Are You Nobody?

PAUL TOURNIER
VIKTOR E. FRANKL
HARRY LEVINSON
HELMUT THIELICKE
PAUL LEHMANN
SAMUEL H. MILLER

PREFACE BY KYLE HASELDEN

JOHN KNOX PRESS
RICHMOND, VIRGINIA

The essay by Harry Levinson is reprinted from THINK magazine, published by IBM, copyright 1965, by Harry Levinson. The other essays were first published in *The Christian Century* and are used by permission of the Christian Century Foundation. The essay by Helmut Thielicke is the greater part of a chapter from his book *The Ethics of Sex*, copyright 1964 by John W. Doberstein, and used here with the permission of Harper & Row, Publishers, Inc.

Scripture quotations are from the *Revised Standard Version of the Bible,* copyrighted 1946 and 1952.

Fifth printing 1973

LIBRARY OF CONGRESS CATALOG CARD NUMBER: 66-21649
INTERNATIONAL STANDARD BOOK NUMBER: 0-8042-3356-X

PRINTED IN THE UNITED STATES OF AMERICA

CONTENTS

Preface by Kyle Haselden 7

I. THE PERSON IN AN AGE OF CONFORMITY 11
Paul Tournier

II. THE WILL TO MEANING 23
Viktor E. Frankl

III. ON THE WAY TO THE TOP 33
Harry Levinson

IV. MYSTERY OF SEXUALITY 45
Helmut Thielicke

V. LET'S BE HUMAN 61
Paul Lehmann

VI. IN A TIME OF UNBELIEF 71
Samuel H. Miller

Contributors 79

PREFACE
by Kyle Haselden

We present *Are You Nobody?* in the hope that it will help correct three of the dominant and destructive characteristics of our time: its collectivism, its use of man as a thing, and its preoccupation with the dissection of man and the diagnosis of his ills rather than with the cultivation of persons. In our day the individual disappears not only under the glacial, senseless pressures of rampant historical movements man seems unable to control but also beneath the massive efforts which seek to rescue man from these threats. In the main our view is focused and our good works are concentrated on social structures rather than on persons, on society rather than on personhood.

The greater good for the greater number—a malicious slogan which disregards the rights and dignities of the lone individual—has become the standard of social reform. Everything for men as groups; nothing for the individual man. This mood and mind worship and serve collectivism as certainly as do the social and political systems in Red China and the Soviet Union. Man is a social being; but human society should not be an ant heap. Christian social thought and cultural analysis developed in part in reaction to widespread identification of Christians with nineteenth-century individualism. But by now the point has been established and the issue has become not "Shall it be individualism or collectivism?" but "What shall be the character of collective life?" The question is about man, about personhood. We must therefore become mindful once more of man, of the individual man who is the least yet the greatest unit in society.

This man—the writings of Berdyaev, Buber, Fromm, and others keep insisting—is not a thing, a manipulatable object. He is a living being—rational, spiritual, and on the human plane self-authenticating. The malicious and the beneficial social forces of our day—despite counsel to the contrary—treat this rational, spiritual being as though he were an exploitable, disposable object, as though he were the means to an industrial, political, economic, or military end. The lust for a robot, for a demi-human creature, has not diminished among men even in the highly civilized Western world. In man's continuous battle to be man Christianity must always reserve some of its forces to counter the perennial attacks on the irreplaceable person and his inalienable rights. Therefore these essays are designed to help us see man as man, as subject rather than object, as a being in his own right and by his God's purpose and not a tool or a commodity.

The brokenness of man in our age has been thoroughly diagnosed; what does the Christian faith prescribe for the recovery of the whole man in a fragmented society? The probing, investigating fingers of psychologists, sociologists, theologians, educators, and political scientists have dug, sometimes harmfully, into the deep recesses of man's being. No doubt there are still unexplored mysteries, unexplained illnesses. But has not the time come to seek once more the wholeness of man, to find nuclei around which his scattered selves may cohere so that multipersonal man may once again be a person? Man, being finite, can never achieve complete integrity; his being is never entirely stable and unassailable. Nevertheless, personhood—as other ages proved—is a possibility, and we must seek it. These essays, though they must by necessity deal with man in compartments, have that reason for being. They seek the recovery of the whole man.

I *The Person in an Age of Conformity*

BY PAUL TOURNIER

It is generally admitted that though he is famous as the inventor of printing, Gutenberg did not in fact invent that art; it was known before his birth in 1397. But his merit is not the less on that account, for it was he who *perfected* printing. The value of an invention is not apparent until it has been developed to the point where it can be incorporated in machines. The outstanding characteristic of the machine is that it lends itself to continual perfecting; this capacity is what ensures its development. Hence also the fascinating attraction of all technology: since every machine is infinitely perfectible it poses new problems for man. The joy he finds in solving these problems arises from the fact that their solution requires a combination of what Pascal called the spirit of subtle ingenuity and the spirit of geometry—a creative idea originating in the realm of intuitive imagination and rigorous thought of the nature of mathematical reasoning. Thus the machine is a witness to man.

Since Gutenberg's day printing machines have been steadily improved. That is why these lines that I write in the solitude of my study can be put into print. I am alone, free, responsible in writing this article, but I am indebted to the machine for its diffusion. The several thousand copies of it that are printed do not differ from this manuscript which I write by hand, with my brain and my heart. But its reach is amplified. The case is the same in all the other domains where machines, more and more perfected, multiply a reality whose source is always personal, in man. The machine enlarges man's field of action, but what it produces depends on him.

Now, what is it that is printed and thus diffused? Do I write in a personal or an impersonal manner? I can write impersonally, in a manner abstract, intellectual, theoretical. I could, like so many authors (more European than American authors, to be sure), enter a complaint against the machine. I could denounce its dominance and its all-pervading influence in our modern world; I could say that it dehumanizes, depersonalizes that world, that in this age of the machine one can no longer be a person. But if I want to be really personal I must rather talk about my own experiences, about my own life. Well, I am aware that up to the age of 34 I was a very impersonal man, a man who delighted in abstract intellectual discussions for the simple reason that I did not dare reveal to anyone else my most intimate anxieties, my most personal emotions, my most secret pangs of conscience. Obviously, the pervasiveness of the machine had nothing to do with that. The problem of the person is eternal. The obstacle is not in things but in ourselves. For each of us the problem is to become more fully a human being, a person. What inhibits us in this attempt is not the external world, not civilization or machinery, but the difficulty that dogs us all when we want to be completely candid and truthful, when we want to show ourselves as we are.

So the problem lies not in the machine but in man. If we are persons, all the machines we construct and utilize will be expressions of our person. And if we were to destroy all machines or give up using them, if we were to return like Robinson Crusoe to a desert island, we would not for all that be persons in a higher degree. Moreover, it is altogether misleading to praise the good old times as more propitious to the unfolding of the person. From antiquity, we cherish the memory of a few men who because of their extraordinary development as persons have left their mark on human culture—a Socrates, for example: the personal man par excellence, even in his philosophical speculations. But we forget the countless masses of slaves whom ancient civilization condemned to an inhuman and impersonal life. From the Renaissance we cherish the memory of a Leonardo da Vinci, or from the heroic days of America that of a William Penn, a Washington, a Lincoln. But we forget that the freedom of a few to affirm themselves has long had a price: coercion of the many.

It seems to me that the success of the machine, the industrialization of the world, the augmented production that the machine has made possible, the increase in well-being and leisure—that all these changes offer to a growing number of people the chance to become *persons*. This, I believe, is the real meaning of the whole recent labor movement and its demands. Is it not also the meaning of the anticolonial movement, victorious everywhere in the world today?

I have been much impressed by the argument in a book by Louis Armand. In that book—*Plaidoyer pour l'Avenir* ("Case for the Future")—this eminent French engineer shows, enthusiastically, that thanks to the machine humanity will perhaps soon, for the first time in its history, know abundance; that we face the possibility for everyone to eat when he is hungry, to have a roof over his head, clothing to wear, and leisure to enjoy, provided the organization of society and the distribution of wealth overcome their lag in relation to the increase in production. Armand adds that this task of organization poses so many human problems at every level that in the future the "humanists" will have to take their place alongside the technicians and the businessmen in the direction of enterprises. Here, obviously, we have the problem of the person set forth by a technician who is well informed as to the economic evolution of the world. (Incidentally, the "humanists" have returned the compliment by naming Mr. Armand to the Académie Française—the first industrialist to become a member of that august assembly!) I too believe that our era will prove able to offer most people a bigger chance of becoming persons; that is why this seems to me such an exciting time to be alive.

It is evident that if man invents and perfects machines, if he conquers the whole earth and ventures into sidereal space, if he makes himself master of the natural sources of energy, it is because he has been created in God's image; because God has conferred on him a spirit of creativeness, of innovation, and given him the power to dominate nature. But what is God's ultimate purpose in endowing man with such faculties? Is it not to permit him to attain a higher degree of conscious personal liberty—which is to say, to become a person, a being in personal relation with God? Shall we be able to help men grasp the opportunity offered us today? Shall we know how to help them make use of the material progress and the greater freedom brought by our time, to the end that they may become more fully men, instead of sinking into a life of ease and comfort, routine and boredom—an animal existence? For a chance is only a chance, a possibility; what counts is what people make of it. They will have more goods and more leisure—but what will they do with these benefits? Will they become persons, or robots? That depends on what they are in their innermost selves.

I do not believe that man can ever become a robot. I believe that to think he might is to show a lack of confidence in him—and in God. I believe that man will always experience the impulse to be human, will always feel a need to recover that in himself which is authentically human, to guard himself against becoming a machine. If he becomes a machine it is not the machine's fault but his own. Even in a primitive, machineless world he can turn into a robot if he is too lazy to invent, to think personally and boldly. And in the world of machines he has built he can be a person if he controls that world by his personal spirit. The machine is strictly neutral: in itself it neither imperils nor favors the flowering of personhood. That flowering is an interior, spiritual event.

In America I was told that my hearers did not quite

understand what I mean by "spiritual event"; I was asked whether this has anything to do with religion. Well, for people who have been taught religion but have never experienced that personal encounter with God through which man becomes a person, religion itself can become impersonal, more or less mechanical, an ensemble of rites and habits and social conventions. Moreover, it is obvious that there are people who though they do not go to church yet have a sense of the person, who are more interested in the person of others than in ideas and things, who respect the person of others because they themselves have been born into a truly personal life.

By nature, man is not a person; either he is grounded in the mass, he belongs so completely to his clan that he is without personal autonomy; or he achieves such total autonomy that he becomes an isolated individual whose communal relation with others is broken. The person stands in a third attitude which demands a new birth, which expresses itself in two ways: through responsibility and through solidarity. It is in the presence of God that man becomes aware of his personal responsibility, and it is there too that he discovers his responsibility for others.

Now it is precisely to escape from our personal responsibility that we constantly accuse others or the external world or civilization—or the machine. If I cannot tear myself away from television even though I have promised myself to go to bed at a reasonable hour, I can say: "It's TV's fault." Thus I make myself out to be the slave of the machine. But it is not the machine's fault, it is mine; it is I who am responsible for my actions. The machine has enlarged the field of human action; therefore the more man fills his universe with machines, the more important it is that he become a person. We are reminded of a word the philosopher Henri Bergson spoke at the beginning of this century. The "addition to the body" brought by technology, he said, calls for a corresponding "addition to the soul."

What then is to be done? What is the import for the world of persons of this new birth of the impersonal world of things? To an industrialist who has not experienced the world of persons, even human beings, his workers, are things, mere instruments of production; and the workers sense his attitude. But to anyone who has been born into the really human world of persons, even things become in some respects persons. Thus, for a worker who is truly a man the machine he operates in the factory is much more than a machine. He speaks to it, gives it a personal name; it speaks to him, he understands its slightest inflection. For him it is alive, it is a partner in life. The same for a railroad man: his locomotive is much more than a thing; it is a living organism, an extension, an amplification of his person. He incorporates himself in it; he knows its caprices, its fits of temper and stubbornness, its joys.

Or again, for St. Francis of Assisi Brother Wolf, Brother Sun, and Brother Body were persons. He peopled his universe with persons because he himself was fully a person. And with what human tenderness he ministered to the people who crossed his path! Another example: A colleague of mine told me that as a child he went every evening to speak to a certain tree, his great confidant, and told it everything. And still another:

Many people feel the need to give their automobiles proper names. The proper name is the sign of the person. Other people think they can show their personal originality by buying a nonstock auto, a unique model. The fact is rather that they lack originality, since they think they can acquire that quality by the uniqueness of the automobile they own! The man who feels himself to be a person transforms the commonest auto and confers on it a personal quality. Then the machine no longer depersonalizes man; man personalizes the machine. The machine does not dehumanize man except to the degree that man ceases to personalize the world. The problem is always in man himself.

A theologian or a physician may be very learned but altogether impersonal, while an engineer may be very personal. That professor is impersonal who lives only in the abstract world of ideas, who sees his students not as persons but only as learning machines. And the students are well aware of this. But they will respond personally to the teacher who now and then tells them something about his personal life. When they meet such a teacher they will open themselves up to the world of persons, will acquire the sense of personhood, will become capable of remaining persons even in the midst of machines. It is by personal contagion that the sense of personhood is transmitted.

I once participated with other medical men in a discussion of the practice in hospitals of what we might call "medicine of the person." Several of the participants declared that the personal relation between physician and patient plays a most important role in the physician's office, but that a large hospital is too impersonal a machine for such a relation to obtain there. Then Professor Richard Siebeck, head physician at the Ludolf-Krehl-Spital in Heidelberg, one of the largest hospitals in Germany, said: "I think I can say that my hospital is pervaded by a personal spirit, but I believe we owe this almost entirely to a single person—our Sister Superior, who is so profoundly human that everyone whose life she touches feels that he is considered a person, feels himself becoming a person." I am pretty sure that Professor Siebeck himself has something to do with the atmosphere at his hospital; we have often sensed as much in the international but intimate Group on Medicine of the Person among whose members I count so many friends.

Medicine of the person is not a method but an attitude; it depends not so much on our medical views (which are the same as those of all our colleagues in the field) as on our own person, on what we ourselves are, on our stance in life. If we are open to the world of the person we can never regard the patient as simply another case, a machine for digesting, breathing, walking, speaking; rather, we see him as a person with whom we can establish a personal relationship.

Appropriately, we of the Group on Medicine of the Person are convinced that if we ourselves are to become open to the sense of personhood, it will not be enough for us to discuss the idea of the person, nor even to search out the biblical sources of that idea. We must become personal toward each other, must talk about ourselves, about our own lives and experiences and emotions. That kind of personal relation, of course, can never develop in medical conventions, which tend to be rigorously impersonal.

Some days ago I attended a meeting of the Group. Among those present was a psychiatrist, a man a little younger than I, a man of whom I am very fond. On the second evening of the meeting he led the discussion. "The problem that has occupied me most these past months," he said, "is the problem of death. I know very well that in a man's life there are times when his primary problem is that of sex or love or vocation. But there comes a time when the problem of death takes first place and must be faced honestly. We in this group have often discussed death—death in general, death as something abstract. These days, however, I have been thinking about *my* death. I was thinking about it last night before I fell asleep. And during the night I had a dream." (But yes! Psychiatrists do not only listen to the dreams of their patients; they have dreams themselves, and very personal dreams. But they do not generally talk about those dreams to their patients, in order to keep the patients at a distance.) "In my dream," continued my friend the psychiatrist, "I saw myself here, in this group. Paul Tournier was sitting beside me. He leaned toward me and said gently: 'Don't think only of death in general, nor of *your* death, but of *his* death.' . . . And I realized that he meant the death of Jesus Christ."

And then and there, suddenly, the person of Jesus Christ rose up in our midst—not like a far-off and abstract figure, but as one very near and real, the one we are all called to encounter some day. In that encounter is the source of the contagion I spoke of above. Surely it was in such personal communion with Jesus Christ that the Sister Superior of Heidelberg, like the professor himself, received the luminous personhood which sheds its light on all whom they meet. If then this contagion is so necessary today in order that our world, rich in machines, shall not be empty of persons, it is from the church that it must spring.

But things are often very impersonal in our churches today. If we visit them and work in them for a while, we soon feel that nobody is really interested in us as persons, that nobody will open himself to us in a very personal way. This is mainly, I think, the result of age. Like all movements, every church at first enjoys strong internal cohesiveness; the pioneers rub elbows, forge personal bonds with each other. But little by little the newness gives way to tradition, initiative to conformity, personal conviction to precept. It is in the encounter with Jesus Christ that we can recover all our humanity, our youth, our freshness, our sense of personhood. Then, without giving up any part of our science or our machines, we can become physicians of the person—teachers, athletes, engineers of the person. And together we can construct a civilization of the person.

II *The Will to Meaning*

BY VIKTOR E. FRANKL

Central to my psychiatric approach known as logotherapy is the principle of the will to meaning. I counterpose it both to the pleasure principle, which is so pervasive in psychoanalytic motivational theories, and to the will to power, the concept which plays such a decisive role in Adlerian psychology. The will to pleasure is a self-defeating principle inasmuch as the more a person really sets out to strive for pleasure the less likely he is to gain it. For pleasure is a by-product or side effect of the fulfillment of our strivings, and it is contravened to the extent that it is made a goal. The more a person directly aims at pleasure, the more he misses it. In my opinion this mechanism underlies most cases of sexual neurosis. Accordingly, a logotherapeutic technique based on this theory of the self-thwarting character of pleasure intention yields remarkable short-term results. Even the psychodynamically oriented therapists on my staff have come to acknowledge the value of logotherapy, and one such staff member has used this technique exclusively in treating sexually neurotic patients.

In the final analysis both the will to pleasure and the will to power are derivatives of the will to meaning. Pleasure is an effect of meaning fulfillment; power is a means to an end. A degree of power—economic power, for instance—is generally a prerequisite of meaning fulfillment. But while the will to pleasure mistakes the effect for the end, the will to power mistakes the means to an end for the end itself.

We are not really justified, however, in speaking of a *will* to pleasure or power in connection with psychodynamically oriented schools of thought, since they assume that man pursues behavior goals unwillingly and unwittingly and that his conscious motivations are not his actual motivations. Thus Erich Fromm in *Beyond the Chains of Illusion* speaks of "the motivating forces which make man act in certain ways, the drives which propel him to strive in certain directions." But to me it is inconceivable that man can really be driven to strivings; either he strives or he is driven. To ignore this difference, to sacrifice one phenomenon to another, is a procedure unworthy of a scientist; to do so is to allow one's adherence to hypotheses to blind one to facts.

Freud and his epigones have taught us always to see something behind or beneath human volitions: unconscious motivations, underlying dynamics. Freud never took a human phenomenon at face value; as Gordon W. Allport states in *Personality and Social Encounter,* "Freud was a specialist in precisely those motives that cannot be taken at their face value." But are there no motives at all which should be taken at face value? Such an assumption is comparable to the attitude of the man who, on being shown a stork, said, "I thought the stork didn't exist!" Does the fact that the stork has been misused to hide the facts of life from children in any way deny that bird's reality?

According to Freud, the reality principle is an extension of the pleasure principle and merely serves its purposes. But one could just as well say that the pleasure principle itself is an extension of the homeostasis principle and serves *its* purposes. Ultimately the psychodynamic approach views man as a being basically concerned with maintaining or restoring his inner equilibrium and seeking to do so by gratifying his drives and satisfying his instincts. Even Jungian psychology essentially interprets human motivation thus; the archetypes of Jungian thought are also "mythical beings" (as Freud called the instincts). Both Freud and Jung view man as bent on getting rid of tensions, be they aroused by drives and instincts clamoring for gratification (Freud) or by archetypes urging their materialization (Jung). In either case, reality, the world of beings and meanings, is reduced to instrumentalities for getting rid of unpleasant stimuli. What has been eliminated in this view of man is the fundamental fact that man is a being who encounters other beings, who also reaches out for meanings to fulfill.

This is why I speak of a will to meaning rather than a need for or a drive toward meaning. If man were really driven to meaning he would embark on meaning fulfillment solely to rid himself of this drive in order that homeostasis might be restored; at the same time he would no longer be really concerned with meaning but rather with his own equilibrium and thus with himself.

Nor is the concept of self-actualization or self-realization a sufficient ground for a motivational theory. Self-actualization is another phenomenon which can be realized only as a side effect and which is thwarted precisely to the extent that it is made a matter of direct intention. Self-actualization is of course a desideratum. But man can actualize himself only insofar as he fulfills meaning, in which case self-actualization occurs by itself —automatically, as it were. Like pleasure, self-actualization is contravened when deliberately sought after or made an end in itself.

While lecturing at Melbourne University some years ago, I was given a boomerang as a souvenir. In contemplating this gift I concluded that in a sense it symbolized human existence. One generally assumes that a boomerang returns to the thrower; actually it returns only when the thrower has missed his target. Similarly, man returns to himself, to being concerned with his self, only after he has missed his mission, only after he has failed to find meaning in life.

In his doctoral dissertation Ernest Keen, one of my assistants during a teaching period at Harvard's summer session, seeks to demonstrate that the shortcomings of Freudian psychoanalysis are compensated for by Heinz Hartmann's ego psychology, and the deficiencies of ego psychology in turn by Erikson's identity concept. Keen goes on to contend, however, that despite these correctives there is still a missing link in psychotherapy, and that this link is supplied by logotherapy. It is my conviction that man should not, indeed cannot, struggle for identity in a direct way; rather, he finds identity to the extent to which he commits himself to something beyond himself, to a cause greater than himself. No one has put it as cogently as has Karl Jaspers: What man is he ultimately becomes through the cause which he has made his own.

Rolf von Eckartsberg, also a Harvard assistant of mine, has shown the insufficiency of the role-playing concept by pointing out that it avoids the very problem prompting it—that of choice and value. For the question remains: Which role to adopt, which cause to advocate? The same criticism holds for those who insist that man's primary intention and ultimate goal are to develop his potentialities. One recalls the example of Socrates, who confessed that he had within himself the potentiality to become a criminal but nevertheless decided to turn away from such a potentiality.

What is behind all these arguments that man should try to live out his inner potentialities or—as it is sometimes put—to "express himself"? The hidden motive behind such notions is, I believe, to lessen the tension aroused by the gap between what a man is and what he ought to become, between the actual state of affairs and that which he should help secure, between existence and essence, or being and meaning. To say that man need not worry about ideals and values since they are nothing but "self-expressions" and that he should therefore simply embark on the actualization of his own potentialities is to say that he need not reach out for meaning to fulfill or values to realize, that everything is all right as it is. Pindar's injunction, "Become what you are," is thus deprived of its imperative quality and transmuted into an indicative statement, namely, that man has all along been what he should become and hence need not reach for the stars to bring them down to earth, since the earth is itself a star!

The fact remains, however, that the tension between being and meaning is ineradicable in man, is inherent in his humanness. And that is why it is indispensable for mental well-being. Having started from man's meaning orientation, i.e., his will to meaning, we have now arrived at another problem—his meaning confrontation. The first issue refers to what man basically is: oriented toward meaning; the second refers to what he should be: confronted with meaning.

To confront man with values which are interpreted merely as self-expression will not do. Still less valid is the approach which would have him see in values "nothing but defense mechanisms, reaction formations or rationalizations of his instinctual drives"—to use the definition of two outstanding psychoanalytically oriented therapists. Personally I would not be willing to live for the sake of my defense mechanisms, much less to die for the sake of my reaction formations.

To treat a patient in terms of psychodynamic ideas may very well serve the purpose of what I call existential rationalization. If a person is taught that his concern about ultimate meaning is no more than, say, a way of coming to terms with his early childhood Oedipal situation, then his concern can be analyzed away, along with the existential tension aroused by it. The approach of logotherapy is altogether different. Logotherapy does not spare a patient confrontation with the specific meaning which he must act on—and which the therapist should help him find. In his book *Logotherapy and the Christian Faith* Donald F. Tweedie recounts an incident in which an American visitor to Vienna asked me to tell him in one sentence the difference between logotherapy and psychoanalysis—where upon I invited him first to tell me what he regarded as the essence of psychoanalysis. He replied: "In psychoanalysis the patient must lie down on a couch and tell you things which sometimes are disagreeable to tell." And I quickly responded: "In logotherapy the patient is allowed to sit erect but must hear things which sometimes are disagreeable!"

Erwin Straus has rightly stressed that in existential thinking the otherness of the other should not be attenuated. The same holds true for meaning. The meaning which a person has to fulfill is something beyond himself, never just himself. Only if this meaning retains otherness can it exert upon a person that quality of imperativeness which yields itself to a phenomenological analysis of one's experience of existence. Only a meaning which is not just an expression of the person himself can be a true challenge to him. The Bible tells us that when Israel wandered through the desert God's glory went before in the form of a cloud; only in this way was it possible for Israel to be guided by God. Imagine what would have happened if God had dwelled in the midst of Israel in the form of a cloud: rather than leading the people safely, the cloud would have obscured everything and Israel would have gone astray.

Meaning must not coincide with being; meaning must be ahead of being; meaning sets the pace for being. Existence falters unless lived in terms of transcendence, in terms of something beyond itself. Here we might distinguish between pacemakers and peacemakers: the former confront us with meanings and values, thus supporting our meaning orientation; the latter alleviate the burden of meaning confrontation. In this sense Moses was a pacemaker; he did not soothe man's conscience but rather stirred it up. Moses with his Ten Commandments did not spare his people a confrontation with ideals and values.

There is also the appeaser type of peacemaker who tries to reconcile others with himself. Let's face facts, he says. Why worry about one's shortcomings? Only a few live up to their ideals. So let's attend to peace of mind or soul rather than those existential meanings which only arouse tensions. What this kind of peacemaker overlooks is the wisdom of Goethe's warning: If we take man as he is, we make him worse; if we take him as he ought to be, we help him become it.

When meaning orientation becomes meaning confrontation, that stage of maturation and development has been reached where freedom becomes responsibleness. An individual is responsible for the fulfillment of the specific meaning of his own life, but he is also responsible *to* something, be it society or humanity or mankind or his own conscience. A significant number of people interpret their own existence not just in terms of being responsible to some*thing* but rather to some*one*—namely, to God. As a secular theory and medical practice logotherapy must restrict itself to such a factual statement, leaving to the patient the decision whether to interpret his own responsibleness in terms of religion or agnosticism. Logotherapy must remain available to everyone; to this I am obliged to adhere, if for no other reason, by my Hippocratic oath. In any case, logotherapy sees in responsibleness the very essence of human existence, and for that reason the patient must himself decide for what and to what, or to whom, he is responsible.

A logotherapist is not entitled consciously to influence the patient's decision as to how to interpret his own responsibleness or as to what to embrace as his personal meaning. The fact that a person's conscience is subject to error does not release him from his obligation to obey it; existence involves the risk of error. He must risk committing himself to a cause not worthy of his commitment. Perhaps my commitment to the cause of logotherapy is erroneous. But I prefer to live in a world in which man has the right to make choices, even if they are wrong choices, rather than one in which no choice at all is left to him. A world in which both fiends and saints are possible is infinitely preferable to a totally conformist, collectivist world in which man is a mere functionary of the party or the state.

III *On the Way to the Top*

BY HARRY LEVINSON

Arthur Robinson, at 34, was energetic, ambitious, neat in appearance, pleasant in manner, and well educated in both management and law. He was chosen over several of his colleagues to become departmental manager. Within six weeks, his superiors observed that despite his experience he was operating in a way which made it difficult to co-ordinate his work with others. Not that he was violating policies and procedures. Rather, without consulting any of his associates, he took actions which disrupted the flow of his department's business. When his boss talked to him about the matter, he seemed to understand the problem, and things moved along smoothly for the next few weeks. But then, he reverted to disruptive actions. Once more, his boss took this up with him. This pattern was repeated over the next several months.

Robinson's superiors were at a loss to understand why a man of high intelligence, qualified by experience and training, and easy to get along with—in short, a man who was ideally ready for this promotion—should fail.

Had their decision to promote him been wrong? Reluctantly, they removed him from his post.

And Robinson, how must he have felt about his failure? What had appeared to be an opportunity turned out to be a setback.

But isn't the American way aimed at trying to get ahead—and stay ahead? Young men everywhere pursue opportunity. Undeterred by such forbidding phrases as "organization man" and "pyramid climbers," their slogan might well be "The future belongs to those who work for it."

Opportunities for growth are highly desirable. Without them men would stagnate. Without competition they would remain undeveloped. Yet promotion for any given man may not be opportunity. Instead, it may be, like Arthur Robinson's experience, a big step toward failure.

The commonsense questions which determine acceptance or rejection of a promotion are usually fairly easy to answer: Will the increased pay be worth the move? Is this move upward, or will it lead to a dead end? Will it bring me closer to the power center of the organization, or will it give me a better chance to show what I can do?

The more important questions, those which have the most to do with success and failure, are much harder to deal with. These call for what Dr. Karl Menninger has often described as uncommon sense. Much of the time, they are not even formulated as questions because the defense mechanisms each of us uses to maintain our own idealistic picture of ourselves hide from our awareness those aspects of our personalities we are unwilling to face. We go to great lengths to hide from both ourselves and others what we feel are our most painful deficiencies and weaknesses. Sometimes we simply deny what we think are our limitations. (Who has not pitied a man whose aspirations so far exceeded his capacities that his goals were mere foolishness?) Sometimes we try to cover our deficiencies by making extra efforts with the talents we have. (Many men have made important contributions by just such compensatory efforts.)

Contrary to the old maxim, what we do not know about ourselves usually does hurt us. There is no substitute for cold, honest self-appraisal.

What, then, are some important psychological questions a man might ask himself as he considers accepting a promotion? These will have to do with how he handles: his need to love and be loved, his aggressive drive, his feelings about his own wishes to be dependent, his conscience, and his modes of self-control. His triangulating points which confirm his decision are his experiences in the past and the *psychological* specifics of the new position he is being offered.

Our actions and experiences in the past will indicate possibilities for the future because the dominant features of our personalities are relatively enduring. Our characteristic behavior patterns are our preferred, established ways of meeting our underlying psychological needs. Some people are characteristically outgoing; they make friends with almost everyone they meet. Others are more reserved, more controlled in their relationships. Some like to work in a group, others by themselves. Some have very high standards for themselves, others are less demanding of themselves and those around them.

As we look back on our experiences, we can easily describe ourselves in these and many other terms. Our patterns of behavior are enduring, since each person doggedly maintains those kinds of behavior which early in life proved to be most successful for him. Such patterns become our personal trademark—we and others recognize who we are because of the continuity of our behavior. In a sense, we are how we behave, and what we mean by personality is the totality of our needs, feelings, and behavior.

A fundamental axiom in considering promotion opportunities, therefore, is that a man should not accept a promotion which requires him to behave in ways which are quite different from the manner in which he customarily prefers to act.

Consider, for example, how a man handles his need to love and be loved. If he characteristically prefers to be somewhat aloof (that is, to deny or avoid his need to be close to others), he will have difficulty when he accepts a promotion which requires him to work closely with others.

This is a case in point. A man who was promoted to supervising engineer is now in his mid-30's. He had never been married, and throughout his tenure in his organization before his promotion he had had little contact with his family who live less than one hundred miles from his work place. He worked hard in his earlier job, sometimes seven days a week. As a result, he built up a reputation as a fast and effective worker, even though he spent little energy on consulting with his superiors. When he took over his present work group, it became isolated from the rest of the organization. He personally devotes as much energy as ever to his work. He has continued his lone-wolf approach, opposing any attempt at teamwork, and is in constant conflict with other department heads. He knows he is irritating to others but says he does not care. Despite his relative success, as reflected by the profitability of his unit, he has had frequent trouble with customers, over-controls his subordinates, and has had continuous conflict with his superiors. Every three or four months, he threatens to quit. His superiors are almost ready to let him do so the next time.

From this man's own personal history, he himself could readily discern that his characteristic mode of giving and receiving affection is one of keeping his distance. It should have been evident to him that the supervision of others, continued relationships with customers, and teamwork necessary in his new job, all require a man to be closer to other people. Straightforward comparison of his preferred behavior with that demanded by the new job would have told him the fit was a poor one.

Quite another problem exists for the man who so much needs the warm affection of many people close to him that it is difficult for him to exercise power appropriately.

There are many variations between these two extremes. In moving up, will a man be cutting ties to friends and associates? Are such close ties important to him? Will there be adequate replacements if such ties are important? If he denies he needs such ties, or assumes they will continue to be available in his new post, he should carefully double check lest the brilliant attraction of his opportunity obscure the realities of his own personality.

The second major issue, how a man handles his aggressive drive, is one which tends to be greatly ignored in business.

All of us have to deal with our aggressive impulses. Executives must be able to invest considerable energy in their tasks to capitalize on opportunity, to overcome obstacles, and to lead their organizations on. Men who compete for advancement know that they must demonstrate their abilities in their own achievements. In short, there is considerable validity to the belief that a good executive must be aggressive.

Frequently, however, though a man can direct his aggressive impulses into the accomplishment of an excellent, even brilliant job on his own, he fails miserably when he is then promoted and has to work through others. The same drive which stood him in such good stead in his own individual performance cannot easily be transformed into indirect support and guidance of other people who carry on the direct efforts.

To avoid deceiving himself and inviting failure a man should ask himself in considerable detail how he handles his aggressive impulses most comfortably. Does he do best when he can organize and carry out a project firsthand? Does he have trouble when he has to let other people do the task? Does he complain about the need to pay attention to the details of relationships with other people in the organization before plunging ahead?

Some people, such as accountants and engineers, handle their aggressive impulses by tightly structured control of their work. Others, such as some salesmen, do so by vanquishing customers. Still others, such as advertising and public relations men, do so by persuasive efforts. A man considering promotion will therefore have to ask himself what new demands the prospective position will have for handling aggression. Will it be more constricting and therefore will the candidate chafe restlessly? Will it demand more frequent open conflict with others and perhaps be somewhat frightening to a man who needs to be more friendly?

One important consideration here is the focus of aggression: Does a man direct his aggression toward himself and consequently make himself fail? This happens more often than most people realize.

One man, for example, had dropped out of college in his third year, then held a succession of jobs, each lasting from three to six months, quitting each in turn because it did not offer opportunity or because he felt his superiors did not want him to advance. He then became an office manager for the local store of a chain. He was so competent in his job (where he could lean on the boss) that he was soon promoted to a similar job in one of the company's largest stores. There he had to function independently. Though he worked hard and did his job well, in a few short months he made a simple "stupid" error which caused the company to question his integrity, and he was promptly fired. Again he felt he had been done an injustice. What he was unable to see was his repeated pattern of failure and self-defeat.

The difficulties inherent in dealing with both affection and aggression in promotion are reflected in classic managerial failures.

The salesman in his continuous contacts and interchange with others draws on those relationships for much of his gratification and channels his aggression directly into the sales task. As sales manager his contacts are limited to supervising salesmen and his aggressive energy finds inadequate outlet in shuffling papers.

The new plant manager who was formerly directly involved in production not only had worked closely with his men but also did something about the problems on the floor. As plant manager, he is necessarily further removed from his old colleagues and he can no longer directly solve a production problem. When he tries to do so, he avoids the new broader responsibility which is now his.

In each of these instances, sources of affection, regard, esteem, and personal ties are diminished sharply. Avenues for the most direct discharge of aggressions also are narrowed. Taken together, such changes can constitute psychological losses, and if they are experienced as losses, the man who suffers them may well wish he had never accepted the proffered promotion.

The third issue, that of dependency needs, is also unrecognized by many businessmen. Every move upward in the organization structure usually requires increasing independence of thought and action. Most men would say, if asked, that they welcome the opportunity for greater independence. A man can rarely admit to himself that he really wants to remain in a subordinate position for, as he perceives it, that would be to admit failure and damage his self-image. Yet many people neither want nor can handle independent responsibility for their own needs to be dependent on someone else are paramount. In pursuing the satisfaction of these needs they become too preoccupied with pleasing their superiors, are reluctant to make decisions or to act by themselves, and are unable to accept the dependency needs of their subordinates.

The last problem is particularly widespread. Many men have all they can do to cope with their own wishes to be dependent. They dislike intensely having other people depend on them. Consequently they avoid, reject, over-control, or attack their subordinates, to the detriment of themselves, their subordinates, and their companies.

This case is a typical example. A company officer is described by his president as brilliant, hard-working, and generally personable. However, says the president, he is overly influenced by and attentive to the ideas and whims of his superiors. This results in his setting aside important projects to find immediate answers to questions which come from an influential source, even if the issue is unimportant. In contrast, he is close to despotic with his subordinates. Both he and his superiors are in frequent turmoil about his behavior, which changes not at all despite repeated discussion. Given what we know about the relative immutability of characteristic personality traits, his behavior is not going to change.

In considering promotion, a man should take a close look at how he has dealt with dependency needs to date. How much independent action has he really sought in the past? Was he actually more independent each step up the ladder or, despite increasing responsibility, did he subtly continue to lean just as heavily on his superiors or selected subordinates? Did he become increasingly anxious with each promotion? Despite obvious talents which seem to send him forward, would he be far happier being a good contributor than an unhappy, unsuccessful leader?

The fourth major psychological issue to be confronted is the ego ideal, or the image one holds of himself at his future best.

The ego ideal is what a man would like to be if only he could be that competent, and the aspiration toward which he is constantly striving. People often have conflicting images of what they would like to be, some of which are unconscious.

Sometimes men follow a given occupation for many years before deciding it is not for them. A number, for example, have gone from business into the ministry or into professional training of one kind or another. Sometimes the conflict has to do with a man's values. Whatever the reason, if a man is not certain in his own mind that he is following his own basic wishes, then he will have great difficulty in his work.

It is commonplace that some men do what their parents want them to do, rather than what they want to do. Such a conflict is relatively obvious, and therefore fairly easy to deal with. When the conflict is more obscure, it is more difficult to resolve. One way of taking a look at the possibility is to raise the question "Do I want this promotion because of what I want to *be* or because of what I want to *do?*" If a man's motivation is to *be* something, he is likely to be pursuing a will-o'-the-wisp, for usually nothing he attains really satisfies him. If, however, his motivation is to *do*—to sell, to manage, to invent, to cure illness—then the satisfactions lie in the doing and, if he does it well, achievement is a consequence.

Here a caution is required. Conscientious people often feel less capable than they really are. The distance between their ego ideals and their daily performance tends to be astronomical, and therefore the gap between their assessment of themselves and what they really are is too large and therefore false. To avoid depreciating his abilities a man should review what he has done. His past performance will realistically reflect his ability.

There is a second caution. Just as promotion is not necessarily the high road to happiness, so it is not necessarily a threat to happiness. Increasing responsibility does not mean increasing stress for everyone. Some will fail with it, some will thrive on it.

Basically, a man has to ask himself: "Will I continue to be me in this new post, or will I have to be someone or something different?" Such a question is not intended to reinforce a rigid position (once a salesman, always a salesman), or to prevent growth and change, but it is to recognize that although we grow older, wiser, more capable, and more responsible, we cannot and do not change our personalities drastically.

There are two final considerations.

It is not easy for a man to look at himself. If he wants to take a good look at himself, he would do well to talk to someone in whom he can confide, and whom he can trust to help him find honest answers—his wife, his superior, his minister, or a professional consultant.

In the last analysis, he must trust his judgment of himself. Usually, if a man decides a promotion is not for him, then that is the wisest decision for him. Most men know more about how they feel and their assets and limitations than those who seek to persuade them. Even if a man underestimates himself, he has to live with his judgment of himself, and how he feels about himself is more critical in his success or failure than what he is objectively.

IV *Mystery of Sexuality*

BY HELMUT THIELICKE

The meeting of two persons under the influence of eros momentarily throws them both off their usual track. Ecstasy in the sense of being "beside oneself" also means being thrown off the track. This leads us to ask whether this is really a matter of being blindly shifted away from one's self or whether it is rather knowingly coming to one's self. The question could also be framed in this way: Is what happens in the eros encounter a "transformation" of one's essential nature or is it a forming of the self beyond and outside of itself? We should have to say that it is the latter. In other words, the solitary Robinson Crusoe does not, strictly speaking, come to himself.

Here again we come to the mystery of sexuality: just as the mystery of the person is enclosed in the husk of sexuality, so this person comes to himself only *in* sexuality and also becomes the object of its self-knowledge. But since on the other hand sexuality points beyond its physical ingredients, we may say that *mutatis mutandis* this coming to oneself takes place not only in the erotic encounter but also in the agape encounter with other people (in diaconic love, for example, and many other sublimations into which the structure of love can change).

We have intentionally said *mutatis mutandis,* for naturally in both kinds of relationship a self is formed in each case with a different center of gravity, and the one without the other generally leads to an actual self that has imperfect contours (even though some very significant exceptions do occur). It is as if a photographic plate with its still invisible picture were immersed in each case in a different developer containing different reagents, which then have their effect in the different way in which the picture "turns out." Therefore the real image of man emerges only in love of God, the magnitude which encompasses all I-Thou relationships. And connected with this is the fact that a living Christian is freed through his encounter with God to become an "original" person and that in the succession of more original—because they are closer to the Origin—Christians there actually are those persons whom we call "originals," because they are different from mere copies of everybody else (*das Man*) and functions of the *Zeitgeist.*

A woman reveals her essential image, as it "comes out" in the sexual encounter, more than does a man. The reason for this is that the woman is identified with her sexuality quite differently from the man. It is, so to speak, the "vocation" of the woman to be lover, companion, and mother. And even the unmarried woman fulfills her calling in accord with the essential image of herself only when these fundamental characteristics, which are designed for wifehood and motherhood, undergo a sublimating transformation but still remain discernible; that is to say, when love and motherliness are the sustaining forces in her vocation.

The man, on the other hand, invests a much smaller quantum of the substance of his being in the sex community. He has totally different tasks and aims beyond the sex relationship which cause him, to be sure, to come back home to his companion, but only in the sense that he returns home from an outside world that claims a far larger part of his time. The peculiar nature of the man tends to emerge less exclusively in his sexuality; it comes out more strongly in confrontation with what Schiller called "hostile life," in which he must struggle, take risks, scheme, and hunt.

Therefore the wife gives her "self" when she gives herself sexually. She holds nothing back, and precisely in doing this she comes to her self-realization. She gives away her mystery (even—how powerfully symbolic this is!—her maiden name), whereas the husband brings in only a part, a very substantial part but still only a part, of himself. The consequence of this nontotality of the man's sexuality is that the man is not nearly so deeply stamped and molded by his sexual experience as is the case with the woman. And related to this again are three basic features which show the difference between the sexuality of the man and that of the woman.

In the first place, we speak characteristically of the seduction of a girl, but not—at least not in the same sense and certainly not with the same seriousness—of the seduction of a man. The meaning that underlies this usage is probably clear enough after what we have said: to seduce a girl means to bring her to self-abandonment;

it means to characterize, to stamp her by sexual intercourse, and thus to release her from a bond which was decisively constitutive of her essential image. In this way the seduction works against the self-realization which the sex community is meant to bring about.

In the second place, connected with this difference is also the phenomenon of the so-called "double standard of morality." This means that general normative public opinion expects of the woman before marriage an abstention from sex in an altogether different way from what is expected of a man; and that the man, even though he himself may live by other standards, not infrequently demands virginity of his future wife. Perhaps we may say that this disparate evaluation of virginity in man and woman (in other words, this "double standard of morality") does have some basis—which we would not wish to be understood as a legitimation of it!—in the physiological structure of the sex organs: whereas the woman receives something into herself, the male sex organ is directed outward, away from himself; it discharges. The *receiving* of something is contrasted with being *relieved* of something. From a purely physiological point of view, the woman receives something from the sexual encounter (and the medical men point out that this is important even though conception does not take place), whereas the man discharges and thus rids himself of something. The extraordinary force of the symbolism of this disparate physical structure can hardly be evaded.

Thus if we make the physiological element normative we do in fact arrive at the double standard. However, we have already been sufficiently warned to see the dubiousness of this absolutizing of the merely partial, physiological side and to know that it is untenable even in the realm of the purely sexual. In connection with the problem of monogamy we shall have to find out at what place the critical point and therefore the theological problem is to be sought.

In the third place, connected with this basic physical structure is the fact that there is in the man a polygamous tendency but in the woman a monogamous tendency. In the light of our foregoing investigations we can no longer doubt the fact that woman is oriented monogamously and the reason why this is so: the woman, because she is the one who receives, the one who gives herself and participates with her whole being, is profoundly stamped by the sexual encounter. To this extent she is marked by the first man who "possesses" her. One must go even further and say that even the first meeting with this first man possesses the faculty of engraving and marking the woman's being; that it has, as it were, the character of a *monos* and thus tends toward monogamy.

Numerous psychopathological symptoms are determined by this structure of feminine sexuality, which in turn bear witness to this structure. Thus a woman's frigidity as well as the vampire insatiability of the strumpet can be caused by a similar experience in youth (violation or brutality in her first sexual encounter). A case of frigidity with this provenience must then be interpreted psychologically: it can be unconsciously willed and used as a defensive weapon by means of which the woman shuts herself off from further invasions and, so to speak, "plays dead."

Here again the *way* in which such a defense occurs is characteristic of the interrelationship of the physical and the personal. We see this clearly when we observe the corresponding masculine parallel. We have such a case when a man is, for whatever reasons, a chronic antifeminist. Sexually, this results in his continuing—for simple physiological reasons—to make use of sexual intercourse, but the emphasis here is on "use." Thus one refuses ever to allow the woman to enter the personal realm of one's own self in such a way that might result in real community or human partnership, but permits her only to come into the physical forefield of the self by using her for the purpose of an instinctive abreaction.

It is therefore significant that the male nature *can* interpret, or rather misinterpret, the physical realm as this kind of forefield and thus is capable of interpreting sex as a mere accident of the person, not as something which is itself *permeated* with the personal. This indicates how the man is able to escape from being stamped and characterized by the sexual encounter and how it does not touch him at the core of his personality—or *seems* not to touch him.

On the other hand, if the woman is determined by an antimale attitude (for which there may be reasons other than those mentioned above), she defends herself against the invasion of sex by resorting to frigidity; in other words, to sexual anesthesia. Accordingly, she does not think of the physical as a forefield in which she might receive at least a physical satisfaction. Rather in her the physical is so interfused and amalgamated with the personal that she can no longer experience orgasm and resists even the very idea of the physical. If she is married, she may tolerate cohabitation as a duty; but then she not only suffers it as something alien to her person which she must put up with, but also merely endures it physically.

In the light of this peculiar integration of the physical and the personal in the woman and the consequent formative power of the first sexual encounter, we begin to understand why there is an innate tendency toward monogamy: out of the center of her nature the woman strives to make totality of her experience correspond to her total submission to the man. Her goal is to make not only the physical side of the man her own, not merely once or temporarily, but rather to own the man's very self. The motive of monogamy lies essentially in the very nature of feminine sexuality. It lies in the urge toward self-realization; whereas without this *monos*-bond she is threatened with being delivered up to a deep contradiction of her own nature; namely, the cleavage of that which in her is integrated and which as a unity she cannot give up without suffering a trauma at the center of her being. In her the capability of separating the physical from the personal and ignoring the "person" of the man would promote loss of selfhood rather than effect the sought-for self-realization.

In what light, then, does this put what we have called the polygamous character of the man? The difference which we have observed between the sexual nature of the man and that of the woman has already indicated the basis of this polygamous tendency; namely, the relative ability of the man to isolate the physiological realm and thus treat it as accidental. But a partnership which is merely physiologically determined can be exchanged at will, because the phenomena of nature are general, while the person is unique and nonrecurrent. However, if we are not mistaken, what comes out of this sex nature of the man is by no means only a physiologically determined urge to change partners, but also what might be called a general "life urge" to exploit the stimulative value of every kind of change (whether it be a change of scene or a change of activity). Thus in this trend toward change there can be a motive that reaches out for what is human, even personal.

Is there a conceivably adequate form of this masculine polygamy? If it were possible to conceive of the masculine in isolation—which, of course, can be done only by some devious experiment of thought—the question could be answered in the affirmative. Physiologically, at any rate, there would be nothing at all to prevent this form of living; and as far as the personal dimension is concerned, the sex experience could possibly be relegated to the periphery, leaving the core of personality untouched. But this is merely talking in terms of an artificial abstraction. For the fact is that the man "exists" as such only because there is such a thing as "woman"; that is to say, he simply cannot leave out of consideration her existence and therefore her sex nature. And since the woman cannot live polygamously without damage to the very substance of her nature, the man cannot do so either.

The reason for this inability is something deeper than a merely moral reason. By "moral" we would mean that the man did not give way to his polygamous tendency merely out of altruistic considerations. The fact is, however, that because of the totality of sexuality *itself* he cannot give way to polygamy without suffering loss of his own substance. As we have already said, he wants an intact wife for himself; he wants this on the assumption that she alone is able to give him the ultimate sexually, since she has not been "marked" by another man and therefore has no zone within herself which is reserved for someone else. But he can demand the two at the same time—sexual freedom for himself and sexual integrity in his partner—only at the cost of an ethical inconsistency, a profound and hypocritical self-contradiction, which he and society in his name seek to justify with the phrase "double standard of morality."

So monogamy is in the last analysis grounded in the personhood of man, inasmuch as this personhood cannot be separated from the physical realm of sex. Since this separation is seemingly possible in the man but obviously impossible in the woman, monogamy is based primarily upon the wholeness of feminine selfhood. We can speak of masculine polygamy only indirectly and *cum grano salis*, because after all masculinity is a relational term—that is, because it cannot be defined apart from feminine existence (1 Cor. 11:11). Therefore one should guard oneself against saying that polygamy is "natural" for the man. For this would be an illegitimate restriction of the term "natural" to the animal. Rather what is "natural" for the man is his manliness, and this means his relationship to the woman; it means that he cannot define and exercise his own sexuality apart from that of the woman without denying his own manhood. Therefore what is "natural" for the man is not that form of sexuality which is in accord with the man as such, with man in his isolation as an entelechy; this cannot be so, if only because such an artificial "man as such" would be a physical monstrosity. What is "natural" is rather that form of sexuality which is in accord with his relatedness to the woman. Hence polygamy, when it is seen from the point of view of the polar wholeness of the sex mystery, is not in conformity with the masculine nature but rather a denial of it.

Once we see that Christian agape regards this "existence-for-the-other-person" as the foundation of all fellow humanity and that it regards man as being determined by his neighbor, it becomes apparent that under the gospel there is a clear trend toward monogamy. Because the wife is a "neighbor," the husband cannot live out his own sex nature without existing for her sex nature and without respecting the unique importance which he himself must have for the physical and personal wholeness of the feminine sex nature. We have already seen that this postulate of agape does not mean that the sexual is merely to be lifted to a higher ethical plane and thus subjected to regulation from the outside and from above, but rather that it is already in fundamental accord with the law of "mutual compliance" *within* the realm of the libido and thus is really in accord with nature itself. But in spite of this clear affinity of monogamy with the gospel, we have intentionally spoken of a *trend* toward monogamy that comes with the gospel. What we mean to express by the use of this term, which appears to be a qualification, is that monogamy is not simply "given" when one becomes a Christian but rather that it "becomes" the sole form of relationship.

Here it is characteristic that the Bible contains no references to this connection which can be quoted in so many words. The Old Testament does not, since it recognizes polygamy. In the New Testament—except in respect to bishops (1 Tim. 3:2; Titus 1:6-7)—the problem is not mentioned at all. So we cannot speak of there being a "law" that demands monogamy. All the more, then, are we prompted to ask how it was that Christianity arrived at the completely unambiguous decision to give monogamy the prerogative of being *the* Christian form of marriage.

If our statement that the masculine sex entelechy (in contrast to that of the woman) has a polygamous tendency is correct, then the autonomy of eros within a society which is determined by the primacy of the man would lead us to expect a trend toward polygamy. And since long periods of history, including church history, are characterized by the primacy of the man, it is surprising that Christianity very emphatically allowed no room, not even the slightest, for this expected tendency.

The Christian decision in favor of monogamy is certainly not to be explained as a conclusion of a "natural theology." For as a rule natural theology tends to regard what is given and desired as natural, so that one can easily figure out what a male-dominated society would have produced in the way of a "natural theology" on this subject. Since direct biblical injunctions also were not the basis for the formation of definitely monogamous customs, we must suppose that quite different motives were at work. These can be found only in the new Christian orientation of personal community—and thus the marriage relationship too—upon agape. Even in primitive Christianity the undisputed primacy of the man in society and the family was limited by the requirement that man should love his wife (agapan). But agape in its New Testament sense means to exist for the other person and enter into his life in a very realistic (not primarily emotional) way. If this is not to be thought of as being merely a universally human, diluted, and abstract attitude of mind—and what could be farther from the New Testament!—then it implies, as we have said, an acceptance of our actual neighbor as he is and therefore of his sex nature too. If for the woman not to be the sole wife of her husband means to wound her, then agape demands that this must not be inflicted upon her.

The only explanation of Christianity's decision in favor of monogamy which seems reasonable to us lies here and here alone: The appeal to agape, which demands the full acceptance of the other person, causes the husband to deal with his wife as a unique, individual person and thus checks his own tendency toward polygamy. Love in the sense of agape teaches us to understand; it also teaches us to understand the other person's sex nature and then in the light of that understanding to "be there," to "exist," for him.

It is therefore strange to observe how both the eros line and the agape line point to the uniqueness of the sex partner. In both cases this uniqueness becomes a basic consideration. (This is not altered by the fact that we were obliged to conclude that in the realm of eros that uniqueness is desired but "in the long run" never attained.) Eros postulates this uniqueness by its insistence upon a highly specified complementarity. Agape has it as its goal, because the indissoluble bond between the physical and the personal (especially in the woman) implies a single partnership and therefore tends toward monogamy.

With a view to controverting the idea that this uniqueness can be grounded only upon eros, I state in conclusion the Christian antithesis to it: *Not uniqueness establishes marriage, but marriage establishes uniqueness.*

With respect to the positive portion of the statement (that it is the marriage that establishes the uniqueness) the sexual encounter that takes place in the marriage and certainly the children who issue from it "mark" the two partners and make them the "one and only" for each other, so that they exist for each other and become a part of each other's destiny. Through it the wife especially —and indirectly through her the husband—acquires a *character indelebilis* in the sense of belonging to each other permanently. And this is exactly what is meant by the uniqueness which comes into being in the marriage *itself.* As we have seen, the wife who surrenders herself invests her whole self in the community of love. She even gives up her name. And since we were compelled to conclude that this is connected with the congruence of sexuality and personhood, especially in the case of the wife, the uniqueness that arises in love cannot have its source only in eros, but must be grounded essentially in agape, which qualifies eros and gives it meaning and purpose. For only agape—the sole attitude in which the other person is really seen, in which he is seen as one who is dearly purchased, as a "person before God" and as a "neighbor"—takes into account this congruence. And thus it also takes into account the characterizing character of sexuality and causes one to respect that uniqueness which comes into being in the sexual encounter.

In view of this uniqueness that comes into being in marriage (it is really something that "happens" and not a timeless, arithmetical assumption), it is therefore not going too far to speak of the *creativeness* of married love. This creative side is the gift of agape. Luther once defined the love of God as contrasted with human eros in this way: "The love of God does not find that which is worthy of his love, but rather creates it for himself; but the love of man comes into being through the lovableness which it finds." Human love—that is, eros—is dependent upon what is worth loving in the other person; that is to say, upon such immanent values as beauty, character, intellect, and harmonious complementarity. It is therefore dependent upon what is transient and unstable and is subject to revision. Hence it is based upon what is perhaps a highly sublimated self-love; for, after all, this kind of love is directed not to the other person's values "as such" but rather to his value "for me." Thus it has within it the question—and this makes it "questionable" in one sense of the word—of what the other person means to *me* and whether he *still* has any value for me. But the love of *God,* which we imitate in agape, is not based upon the calculable value of the other person for me. For God does not love us because we are so valuable; rather we are valuable because God loves us. Because the other person is valuable to God, he compels me to show reverence. Therefore my love is no longer addressed to an unstable function, to what in any given moment I can or cannot find to be "valuable for me" in the other person. The continuing faithfulness of God with which he is surrounded also makes my relationship to him a continuing one.

Agape therefore penetrates beyond the superficialities of the momentary adequacy or inadequacy of the other person and addresses itself to his ultimate mystery. And this is precisely what makes it creative: the other person knows that he is being addressed and respected at the core of his being, at that point of human dignity which is unconditioned by, and independent of, what he is in actuality and which has its own hidden history with God. In this way agape brings out—"loves" out, as it were—the real person within the other being. This is why all those who came into contact with Jesus—and especially the dubious characters, the harlots and publicans, the outcasts, the outsiders, the insulted and injured—were dignified by his agape and grew up into that dignity. They did not first have to qualify themselves in order to become worthy of this love; rather, they were qualified by this love. And if this is not misunderstood in the sense of idealistic philosophy, one might even say that under the warmth of this love they grew to be something beyond themselves. This love addressed itself to the child of God within them, and therefore it liberated that child of God within them. It was a creative breath that blew upon them. Therefore it is not mere romanticism to dare to say that one can tell by looking at many older married folks that they have been much loved. Qualities have been released within them, "loved out of them," which their own entelechy would never have brought out. This, too, is part of the law of "forming the self" which genuine love carries into effect.

Thus all love in the sense of agape and eros which has been transformed by agape is like a reproduction of that divine creativity which Luther ascribed to the love of God. It is in the light of this creative love that we are to understand the statement that married love creates uniqueness and does not itself arise from uniqueness.

V Let's Be Human

BY PAUL LEHMANN

In my *Ethics in a Christian Context* (published by Harper and Row) I ventured to describe by the phrase "keeping human life human" the biblical account of what God is doing in the world. This concept of God's activity and purpose seemed to accord admirably with what Christian theology has been trying to express through the doctrines of the trinity, the incarnation, the atonement, the "second Adam," and the second advent; thus biblical messianism and christocentric humanism could be seen as of one piece. These phrases denote the specific content of the knowledge of God and of ourselves—which Calvin called "true and substantial wisdom."

However, the phrase "keeping human life human" has apparently raised as many problems as it was intended to settle. What was put forward as a readily negotiable bridge between the tradition of biblical and Christian thought and certain central experiences and problems related to man's understanding of himself and his world failed to carry the load of meaning expected of it. The statement that what God is doing in the world is making and keeping human life human seems not to have conveyed, as was intended, a dynamic, concrete, and self-evident sense of the divine activity and purpose and of man's involvement therein. Instead of clarifying, the phrase has obscured a pivotal concern of Christian theology and ethics. At least one can say that the ambiguity involved in so speaking about the knowledge of God and of ourselves has been insufficiently dispelled.

Certain comments may help clarify the language used in speaking thus of knowledge about God and ourselves. The first concerns our eroded apperception of the human; the second deals with a historical occasion pertaining to the human; the third constitutes a theological consideration of the particular significance of the human for the interpretation of Christian faith and ethics.

G. K. Chesterton once observed that if a man on his way from Lancaster to Reading were to meet a traveler going in the opposite direction the question he almost certainly would ask would be "Who are you?" The likely answer would be "I am a carpenter" (or a tailor, miner, lawyer, and so on). It would, observes Chesterton, almost never occur to anyone to answer "I am a man." It has always seemed to me that Chesterton was underlining the eroded apperception of the human so widely and increasingly prevalent in the culture of our time.

The ambiguity afflicting the phrase "to make and to keep human life human" as it applies to God's activity and purpose in the world is rooted in the fact that "human" is no longer a self-evident characterization of man's experience and of his awareness of himself in the world. Since what was once considered obvious has become problematical, we are compelled to explain to ourselves who we are. The laboriously wrought achievements of the human spirit—whereby from the dawn of animism onward the consciousness of self took shape within the formative power of consciousness at work upon the "womb of nature"—have fallen into disarray. As W. H. Auden has put it, "the pilgrim way has led to the abyss." Man, Auden declares, sees himself as having the power to explain "every what in his world but why he is neither God nor good."

The apperceptive character of the disintegration of which I write is perhaps most vividly evident when one considers the basic function of language in the guarding and the shaping of man's awareness and understanding of who he is. Just as language forms the structure of human self-discovery and self-communication, so grammar forms the structure of language. Thus application of the techniques of grammar should make it clear that "human" is the adjectival form of "man." But the adjective has lost its appropriate noun and now sits loosely upon a congeries of possibilities, pointing to nothing so much as a disturbing vacuum at the center of man's attempt to report on himself. He speaks of "human" possibility, "human" creativity, "human" achievements, "human" failures, "human" goodness, "human" suffering—even of "human" engineering. In each case the "human" is defined with reference to considerations which are for the most part other than man himself or man's chief end. To define the "human" with reference to itself is to involve definition in tautology—and tautology constitutes the perfect formula for meaninglessness. This is what we have in the case of "making and keeping human life human." Thus the phrase is not only not illuminating; it is at best confusing, at worst empty.

Grammar, however, has to do with the structure of language, not of logic. As such, it opens the way to a function of tautology other than that of signaling the absence of meaning, and in so doing it places logic at the disposal of human self-discovery and self-communication. In this case, tautology signals not the absence of meaning but the limits of logic in giving meaning to man's experience of himself and of his world. Where man is concerned, tautology constitutes a marker on the boundary between logic and life. To use the expression "making and keeping human life human" is a tautological way of speaking. But now the tautology marks and guards the entrance into the territory of human self-discovery and self-communication where man simultaneously *reports himself* and *reports on himself.*

The grammatical symbol of this double focus is the functioning of "human" both as adjective and as noun. As an adjective "human" says something about man; it is like saying that he is wise or foolish, weak or strong, animal or machine. As an adjectival noun "human" says something about man in such a way as to include man himself in the very act of speaking about him; it expresses the mystery and the obviousness of the discrete creature that man is. Thus to speak truly about man is to speak in such a way as to make plain that what is said about man coincides with what man says about himself. When, then, we venture to describe what God is doing in the world in terms of his purpose and activity "to make and to keep human life human" we are expressing a tautology that derives its meaning from the double focus hidden in the use of "human" as an adjectival noun. The primary question then becomes not whether this is a meaningful way of speaking, but what *is* the meaning the adjectival noun discloses.

The question concerning "the human" is thus interchangeable with "What does it mean to be man?" when that question is asked with the simple, concrete, and full sense of the word "man" in mind. It is this question which Kierkegaard was seeking to underline by his dictum that "truth is subjectivity," which he endeavored to explore through an analysis of the paradoxical mode of truth. This is the question we have unlearned to ask in our time. Not that we have ceased to utter the words; rather, we use them with insufficient attention to the tautological signals. The words have lost their sense for us because we have lost our apperceptive sense of direction.

In one issue of the *New Yorker* there appears a cartoon picturing a man whose head is caught in a coil spring of his own designing and whose entire body seems likely to be drawn irresistibly into the device. The single focus has displaced the double, the "human" has become the mechanical. The drawing bears no legend; language has lost its apperceptive function as a means of communicating the "human." More than two decades ago W. H. Auden anticipated this eroding of an apperception of the human:

O how the devil who controls
The moral asymmetric souls,
The either-ors, the mongrel halves
Who find truth in a mirror, laughs.
Yet time and memory are still
Limiting factors on his will;
He cannot always fool us thrice,

For he may never tell us lies,
Just half-truths we can synthesize.
So, hidden in his hocus-pocus
There lies the gift of double focus,
That magic lamp which looks so dull
And utterly impractical
Yet, if Aladdin use it right,
Can be a sesame to light.*

Long before Kierkegaard tried to stem the erosion of our apperception of the human, Socrates had launched a way of thinking that put man in the center of reflective attention. In so doing he gave philosophic pre-eminence to the animistic gropings and insights of the past and set philosophy in a new key. The enormous importance of the Socratic revolution, not only to the Western intellectual tradition but for the understanding of the mind of man itself, can scarcely be overestimated. Its central insistence was that Socrates' predecessors had been asking the wrong question, the wrongness consisting in their tendency to ask a proper question in an improper way.

To ask "What is the nature of things?" prior to and in disregard of the question "What is the nature of *human* things?" is to put the cart before the horse on the philosophic road. If one wishes to understand and to interpret reality (being and knowing, as Socrates would have said), one must first understand that thinking is an activity of man, then recognize that truth is intrinsically and fundamentally a relation between the knower and what he knows, between man and the object (or end or aim) of his reflective activity. Thus "Know thyself!"

* From *The Double Man*, by W. H. Auden. Copyright 1941 by Random House, Inc. Quoted by permission.

became the primary axiom of philosophy, and understanding the human became the prerequisite to understanding everything else. The gift of double focus which hitherto had been unable to provide the clarity of sight which would give order to man's experience of himself and his world—with their unity and change, pride and nemesis, guilt and atonement, vice and virtue, fate and promise of fulfillment—became "a sesame to light." "That magic lamp which looks so dull and utterly impractical" had found an "Aladdin" to "use it right."

The fruit of the Socratic revolution was basically an apperceptive discovery which Socrates identified as "the primacy of soul" and which he explored as an adventure into the context and the implications of "the soul's surmise." His inquiries took him through the streets of Athens as well as through the labyrinthine recollections of the soul. And he drew men into a way of thinking about life and of living life which distinguished knowledge from opinion and ordered appetite by reason, and which conjoined truth with goodness, self with society, responsibility with well-being, and the wholeness of man with the beatific vision of the harmony of the spheres. To ask, in such a context, what it means "to make and to keep human life human" is to engage in the sophistry of claiming not to know, when what is really lacking is a sense of the prerequisite for knowing anything at all; what has been exposed is not a default of knowledge but a defective apperception.

Understanding the human with reference to the context and implications of the Socratic revolution is particularly instructive because in this context the apperceptive aspect of the question concerning the human is clearly and meaningfully exposed. One is not limited, however, to the Socratic context so long as one does not ignore the Socratic lesson. Socratic humanism is a profound and all but indispensable way of explaining what it means "to make and to keep human life human." If Socratic humanism is nevertheless to be set aside, the reason can be only that its apperceptive discovery is more faithfully exhibited in another context: the apperception of the human provided by and derived from the truth and life that are in Jesus Christ.

For the present purpose this context may be called "Christian humanism" to distinguish it from "Socratic humanism." It must be recognized, of course, that the cultural history of the two is inextricably intertwined; neither has come to pass or managed to survive without the other—this is part of the story of erosion already referred to. Nevertheless there is an important line of demarcation between Christian and Socratic humanism which can be discerned through their respective contexts. The line of demarcation is drawn by the conjunction between semantics and salvation.

With regard to the apperceptive prerequisite for understanding what it means "to make and to keep human life human," the *language of the human* is the same for those who have been taught primarily by Socrates as for those who have been taught primarily by Jesus. Questions of chronological priority or of logical dependence or independence, as between Socrates and Jesus, are beside the immediate and crucial point at issue here: that the *language* of the human and the *description* of the human are not the same. The context and implications of Socratic humanism are different from those of

Christian humanism. The difference concerns not the fact of the apperception of the human but the roots of this apperception, the way in which its prospects of fulfillment in human experience are assessed, the depths of its failure to shape the living of human life, the power to persevere in the responsibility for what the humanity involves.

To go back to Calvin, for example, it makes a not inconsiderable difference in the content of that "true and substantial wisdom" by which the life of man in the world is informed and guided whether that content is described in terms of the knowledge of God and of ourselves or in terms of the knowledge of the divine in ourselves. The difference is considerable because both the meaning and the power of being human, and of being fulfilled without becoming other than human, are affected by that to which the language of the human refers. The particular truth and significance of biblical and Christian faith and ethics lie in their insistence that the semantics of the human and the salvation of man belong together. Apart from the salvation of man, the language of the human loses its denotative referent; apart from the language of the human, the salvation of man loses its connotative possibility.

When the activity and purpose of God in the world are described as "God's doing what it takes to make and to keep human life human," the language of man with regard to himself and man's experience of himself begin to coincide. Then the truth and the life that are in Jesus Christ begin to give shape to and to take shape in man's consciousness of self without self-consciousness, in man's acceptance of his neighbor—not as an "I-Thou" but as himself, in man's dominion over the world as the servant of the God who beheld everything that he had made as "very good" and who gave to man the gift of being human as the peculiar and concrete mark of his creaturehood. As regards what it means to be human and to gain the power to stay human, Jesus Christ is the "wisdom of God" and the "power of God" (1 Cor. 1:24). He is "the truth [that] will make [men] free" (John 8:32). In him men are already on the way toward being fully human—that is, whole, complete in themselves because completely related to their kind and to everything that God has made. Thus to be human is to be what God made and purposed man to be, and to exhibit the fact that God's chief purpose and man's chief end are identical.

VI *In a Time of Unbelief*

BY SAMUEL H. MILLER

Today the assumption is widespread that believing has fallen on evil days. Modern man has brushed the cobwebs from his mind, cast off ancient illusions, and looks now with honest realism at the world in which he lives. His sophistication is antiseptic, washing everything clean of any superstition or superfluous meaning or religious inference. Science has trained us all to be wary of overtones or exaggerations; we believe only what we can prove—the rest is sheer self-deception. This is the age of unbelief!

There is plenty of evidence to buttress such a position. For a century or more we have heard of the "death of God" in such a chorus of voices philosophical, religious, and literary that only a bishop could have made a best seller out of the news—and if God is dead, what is there left for a man to believe? Moreover, the great structure of Christian dogma has fallen into ruin during the past three centuries, having been demolished by the sciences through a series of relentless attacks on all sides until the only hope of the faith is to cast off its mythological garb and assume an existential pose—so if the grand scheme of Christian truth is no longer valid, what is left for believing? And on top of all that, it is being assumed in many quarters that we have now reached the time when the church is no longer necessary for religion, inasmuch as the world has grown up and can read the signs of grace in history without the supporting counsel of the church—churchless Christianity, it is called, now a popular movement in Japan but with not a few followers in many other places. The stage is swept clean, and we are ready for another act—but what part the believer is to play in it is not plain. He would seem to be little more than a quaint anachronism.

That the believer is embarrassed in this modern world is rather obvious. Both the innocence of ritual and the ritual of innocence have been lost in the sharp teeth of our hypercritical faculties. We have probed and penetrated, observed and analyzed, tabulated facts and gathered data, until it seems that whatever escaped us could be scarcely more than a shadow, perhaps no more than the shadow of our own hands, but certainly nothing real. No one has ever put it more simply than did Freud: If science cannot discover it, it just isn't there!

Certainly the strain on *believing* is heavier than ever before. We have pushed the structure of relationships further in all directions; we *understand* more than ever before; we will not rest content until we can corner the obscurity, X-ray the darkness, and discern the connections. We are impatient with mystery, skeptical of anything we cannot measure or isolate. All of which means we do not like questions framed in such a way as to make it difficult for us to find answers; we turn the questions around to fit the kind of answers we can find. As for the naïve language of space and power by which we once described God, it leaves us embarrassed now, yet we find no easy substitute. The radical subtlety of religious realities puts a new burden on believing.

But these very facts—our clear seeing, our fundamental realism, our skeptical judgment, our loss of innocence and repudiation of credulity, our mature sophistication and refusal to be taken in—all are the very factors which make it increasingly impossible to confuse real believing with its counterfeits. The profoundest belief comes only with the most sophisticated minds. There is no better example of this than Søren Kierkegaard, whose penetrating analysis of the inadequacy of Hegelian rationalism is accompanied by the most passionate believing. Or similarly, the astute genius of a Pascal, whose clear distinctions still provide us with profound perspectives. Or even better, the example of Christ Jesus. Here one can only measure the most penetrating skepticism about the contemporary convictions of his day and the amazing simplicity of a profound faith. In our day the very factors that seem to have made this an age of unbelief are those which support the integrity of believing. Believing has been pushed from its false premises to a frontier where the contrast is stronger and the decision clearer.

If we continue to regard belief as a kind of variable, fluctuating with each age, rising and falling like the tide, the truth is, it seems to me, that we do not understand the situation in regard to man's believing. Believing is as much as an integral factor in man as are eating and sleeping. It is intrinsic to his nature. He neither gains nor loses faith; he merely changes the object of it.

Indeed, he believes in the most outrageous things. Under the mixed signs of romanticism and reason he has believed in Utopia, in the French Revolution, and in Brook Farm. Believing is as inevitable as breathing. One way or another he believes, negatively or positively; if not in heaven, then in hell; if not in God, then in fate; if not in fate, then in law; if not in law, then in aimless chance.

Under the charismatic Führer he believed in Aryan supremacy and the mass extinction of Jews. He believes in vegetarianism, reincarnation, the existence of people on other planets, ouija boards, infallible scriptures, salvation by psylocorbin drugs, free enterprise. There is little or nothing that man, even modern man in all his supposed sophistication, will not believe. Man is simply an inveterate, incurable, inevitable believer. Sometimes what he believes in makes sense, and at other times it does not. No matter: he must believe. And if not in a reality that reason points to, then in a fantasy which his reason will rationalize. Believing is the act by which he relates himself to history, the act of interpenetration, the act most human whereby he invests himself in the meaning he perceives or imposes on the stream of events which bears him down the stream of time. Nor does he hesitate to "mythologize" science, politics, race, or business.

Indeed, utterly wrong, it seems to me, is the traditional notion that man begins his relation to the world and history in reason and that when reason can carry him no further and he still seeks to extend his experience he relies on faith. Believing is prior to reason: it is fundamental to it and sustains it. Man is basically a believer, and only as he is a believer is he a reasoner.

Probably the most radical problem of our time is not so much the effort to demythologize the New Testament as the far-advanced demythologizing of man himself. Those dimensions of his own being which correspond to the nature of myth in the tradition of faith have been held in contempt and have rapidly fallen into atrophy. Other levels of experience have become so favored, the traffic of idea and activity has become so channeled, the energies have been so attracted and expended in special ways that the larger perspectives and magnitudes of thought and sensibility have been evacuated and great stretches of roads and towns, once busy with life, are now empty except for the hollow echoes of ghostly memory.

Another way of saying this is to draw attention to the interesting way in which the center of believing has moved from the focused center of the church to the more generalized area of secular activity in the world. Nowhere is this more intensely and blatantly illustrated than in the sphere of politics. Believing, in its most serious sense, which has been associated traditionally with heresy and orthodoxy, is no longer bitterly contested in the religious realm; heresy and orthodoxy are not sharply discriminated, and they no longer arouse intense anger or fanaticism in the religious community. But in politics they do: tolerance and humor tend to vanish; angry citizens draw up petitions demanding the dismissal of professors who dare to sponsor a candidate of the opposite political party. As for the conflict with communism, there is no limit to either the paranoid suspicion or the fanatic hatred which it has engendered. Believing in the political arena has become the act of absolute judgment, of heresy and orthodoxy, of demonic fears and inquisitional ethics. Read in the light of older events in ages of absolutism, the political trials, confessions, and manipulations take on an entirely new aspect—all the symptoms and syndromes are there but under political signs. Believing has become secularized, or politicized. It has its own *mysterium tremendum,* its own numinous aura, its own sanctity and blasphemy.

There is a great mystery in man the believer. He does not so much believe when the way is open and made easy. It is only in the pinches, when life forces him against the wall, when all the odds are against him, when there is no reason at all to believe that he does believe. He believes when everything is against belief. One is reminded of Camus's remark about the existentialists. "It is strange," he says, "that works like those of Kafka, Kierkegaard, and Chestov . . . completely oriented toward the Absurd and to consequences—should in the long run lead to that tremendous cry of hope." Call it hope if you will; it is faith, too. It is the cry which evinces man's freedom, his reach beyond despair, his believing—the sign and gesture of a transcendent reality in himself. Man simply cannot submit to the Absurd as the final dimension in reality; his own voice utters a word beyond the Absurd—a word of mystery, to be sure; of dignity always; and in truth the celebration of a joy that reverberates through the silences of sea and sky until creation itself gathers new meaning. Man the believer is the first Adam who discovers in his fall the negative reach of the spirit; man the believer is the second Adam who discovers in Christ the positive reach of the atonement, in which the highest and the lowest, the sublime and the common, the ultimate peace and the deepest suffering are all brought together.

CONTRIBUTORS

PAUL TOURNIER is a physician and clinical psychologist in Geneva, Switzerland.

VIKTOR E. FRANKL is Professor of Neurology and Psychiatry at the University of Vienna medical school and head of the neurological department of Vienna's Poliklinik hospital.

HARRY LEVINSON is a psychologist with the Menninger Foundation.

HELMUT THIELICKE occupies the chair of theology and is dean of the theological faculty at the University of Hamburg.

PAUL LEHMANN is Auburn Professor of Systematic Theology at Union Theological Seminary in New York.

SAMUEL H. MILLER (1900-1968) was dean of Harvard Divinity School.

KYLE HASELDEN (1913-1968) was editor of *The Christian Century*.